My
Life with
Sydney Laurence

My Life with
Sydney Laurence

by Jeanne Laurence

A SALISBURY PRESS BOOK
A division of Superior Publishing Company
Seattle, Washington

DEDICATION

TO MY HUSBAND

SYDNEY LAURENCE

Foreword

HOW can one do justice in words to a work of art done on canvas? There really isn't anything left to say after the artist has done all the saying. Neither clever phrases or fancy superlatives will help the painting one bit. But if it has moved one beyond ability of expression, appreciation of the best is shown in one's purchase of it. Time and again this happened in Alaska with the miner, the fisherman, even the doctor, lawyer and Indian chief who spent their last silver dollar on a painting so they could have great art on their cabin walls.

Great art on cabin walls? Open for question, an outsider would say and wonder what would a miner or fisherman or layman know about art anyway. Truth is that the outdoor man in Alaska lives art in observation of it everyday —the color of the sunrise and sunset, the true tone of the Northern Lights, the brightness of moonlight on the silent snow.

Art in Alaska was born with the primitive Eskimo who carved beauty and human interest into his living things called artifacts today. Likewise has the Indian left traces of his early culture in things of exquisite beauty. Then followed the scrimshaw art of the early Arctic whalers who in their spare time expressed what is always deep in the soul of man. But the man who came to Alaska with the early day gold seekers was the first to paint in Alaska and document his great and inimitable works with his signature—Sydney Laurence.

Alec Bowne of Cash Creek tells of first meeting him up on the Yentna. "He was living in a little 'ol tent and painting little 'ol pictures not much larger than a two dollar bill. Sketches he called them . . . thought he was a queer duffer then cause he looked strong enough to work. But later when I saw what he'd done with those sketches that really opened my eyes. It was the grandest sight I had ever seen—painted right here in this studio. Just took my breath away—a huge painting of Mt. McKinley, and you know, that painting he sold for fifty thousand dollars and it hangs in the Smithsonian Institution today."

Alec continued with personal things about Sydney who never forgot the miners and prospectors he met out on the trail around the Peters Hills where he did much of his outdoor painting. Whenever these men came to town they would be his guests no matter what was going on at the time. Walking and looking the studio over Alec remarked, "Same parlor, bedroom, woodshed, kitchen and all, and he had that big north light put in to bring plenty of light in for painting his big pictures. Must be a pleasure to work here where his greatest work was done." It was more than a pleasure and I held great hopes of meeting Sydney Laurence some day. We heard he was painting in Europe during those days of 1916.

Not until the early thirties did I meet him—a day long to be remembered in meeting him and Jeanne too. Right away I was taken to his studio and what a sight I did see. Reproductions of his Mt. McKinley paintings were familiar to me but now I saw his originals—marine and hill and mountain scenes all rich in color and beautiful in tone. But I have no words to describe these first originals I saw that day in his studio or should I try as each painting spoke of things this master, who always mixed feeling with medium, was successful in getting across to the connoisseur, the native or the common man on the street.

"Let's have a snort," he said drawing me away from his work. Salutations followed, then, altruistically, he welcomed me into his bailiwick. Suddenly his keen eye caught something out of the window "By gosh!" he exclaimed, "Spring is actually here. See that fresh green on the stand of birch out there?" More than a mile away, and too faint for most eyes to see was the fresh green touch of Spring. He got those tones which others exaggerated—if they saw them—but never did he find it difficult to arrive at truth. The natural came easy for him to paint so naturally he could not paint the off-key unnatural.

Meeting Sydney and Jeanne was like stepping into the home of someone I had known all my life. I was invited to have dinner with them and their friends on the following night. An incident took place as we were about to eat which could have been most embarrassing had it happened elsewhere. Sydney's plate was passed to him, then it happened—too quick for the eye to see as it fell against him, flip over to land bottom up with all the food on his lap. Jaws dropped in stricken fear. The food was hot but he made no sudden movement of pain. Calmly he pointed a knowing finger at me and said, "I did that once before—at the Salmagundi Club." It brought a roar of laughter from all, even from those who knew not of this most exclusive of clubs in America.

Sydney could size up character in one at a glance but that glance was sharp and penetrating to the bone and marrow. "Oh God! look at what's coming. You're in for it but not me," he said as we once sat talking in the lobby of the Anchorage Hotel. It was a noisy man who walked up to us and described a sunset he had seen. "Yessir Sydney," he said, "You should have been there to paint it. It was pink and orange and—" He didn't finish. Sydney, fumbling with his pocketed ear phone battery said "It's not working today—out of commission" whereupon the man left allowing Sydney to say, "You should get one of those for your left ear. Keeps you from getting awful tired. That big mouth is an impossible bore—a four hundred pound horse-power ass."

He pronounced Seward as Surred. "Got a wire from Surred." he said one evening "Would you like to go down to the station in the morning and meet a bunch of women for me? They want to come to the studio . . . tourists from the states . . . school teachers probably . . . might sell them a stinker size. . ."

"You might sell them a big one Sweety" said Jeanne.

Gladly I went to the station next day and brought them to his studio. He was reading "The Arts" by van Loon when they entered to shake his hand and introduce themselves—five school teachers in all who were thrilled beyond words over their trip to Alaska and meeting Sydney Laurence.

I was about to leave but Sydney motioned me to stay which I did being more than eager to observe his manner in salesmanship. I had been to many

8

exhibitions to find the approach of all artists different but his was far from different, it was strange—as if he wasn't in the room at all though he came forward quietly to answer questions in his gentle and natural way. At times I felt a sale was slipping—that a certain word spoken would bring attention back to a painting as the tourists went on to study the next subject. But it took me some time—many days later, to fully realize I had seen a master salesman in art operate. It was Sydney's whole nature, his great simplicity that came out which was that he did not try in the least to sell for if his work couldn't sell itself he felt it wasn't good work. Yet he never had a painting that didn't sell.

"I told you Sweety you would sell a big painting and you sold three," said Jeanne after the ladies left. But I was the only one unhappy about the sale. I never liked having to see his paintings leave Alaska.

In his heyday he brought more people to the Territory than any one man. All who had seen his great work wanted to meet him as well as to see Mt. McKinley often publicized as the highest mountain in the world which it is from its immediate base. His greatest McKinley now hangs in the Whitney Gallery of Western Art at Cody, Wyoming and has recently been appraised at $200,000.00.

Often the subject keeps coming up of changing the name of McKinley back to its old indian name—"Denali—The Great One." The change would be appropriate yet as appropriate and far more colorful would be the name of the man who blazed a trail of beauty in Alaska for all coming artists to follow.

C. Heurlin
Ester, Alaska

I am grateful to these people, owners of Sydney's paintings, who have assisted me in the collection of pictures which this book contains, they are listed in alphabetical order with the page numbers on which their paintings appear.

Jeanne Laurence

My Life With Sydney Laurence, A Great Man

BY JEANNE LAURENCE

NO doubt the wonder years of my life and the happiest ones were spent with my husband, Sydney Laurence, whom I met through mutual friends, a Mr. and Mrs. Lou Sidell, who had an art store across the street from my Los Angeles studio. From early morning until late afternoon, often as late as seven o'clock, I was at work painting.

One day Edith Sidell said to me, "Don't you ever go out? All we see is you at work." "No," I replied. "I always have so much work that it keeps me busy filling orders." "Well, you should go out from time to time." "I would like to very much if I could find someone about ten to fifteen years older than I." I always looked much younger than I was and I only met men my age or younger than I. I wanted to meet someone quite a bit older. Both Edith and Lou said, "We have a good friend, who happens to be a neighbor of yours, a Sydney Laurence who just recently came from Alaska. We will give him a call and find out if we can bring you over to meet him." They called Sydney and he said, "By all means, I will be very happy to meet your friend" and they made an appointment for that same evening.

When we met we immediately took a liking to each other; one could almost say it was love at first sight. After a very enjoyable evening my friends brought me to my door and asked me if I would look in on Sydney once in a while. Having come so recently from Alaska and not knowing anyone in Los Angeles, he was quite lonely. I promised I would.

The next day I called Sydney and asked him to come to dinner, which invitation he accepted. That was the beginning of our romance. He enjoyed the dinner very much as he was tired of eating in restaurants all the time. From then on I went home earlier and cooked dinner; I would then go to his door and knock and ask, "Sydney, will you come and share dinner with me? I always cook more than I can eat." "Under one condition," he replied, "and that is that you will go to the movie with me." I told him that would be a pleasure as I was very fond of shows.

At the time I met Sydney he was not too well; he had a heart condition and had to see the doctor about once a week. As days went on his health improved and the doctor, who had given him just a short time to live, wondered about his improvement and asked him, "What are you doing? Each time you come for a checkup your health has much improved." Sydney told him about the French girl, a neighbor that he had met, who asked him to dinner every day. He told the doctor that from that time on he began feeling better day by day. "She is a mighty good cook," he said. "and I enjoy my meals with her very much." The doctor then said, "The next time you come bring her along; I would like to meet her."

When I went with Sydney, Dr. Tardini asked me if I had relatives in San Pedro by the name of Picherie and some in Los Angeles by the name of Lees. I told him that I did and that Mr. Lees was my mother's brother and that his daughter, Mrs. Picherie, was my cousin. "I thought so," said the doctor. "Every time the Lees or the Picheries come for a visit they talk about their cousin Jeanne from France and praise her cooking." Dr. Tardini took me aside and asked me if I would do him a favor and keep on cooking for and looking after Sydney the way I had been doing. He said that his health had improved so much since the day he started eating his dinners with me, adding "You could prolong his life by ten years." I gave the doctor my promise to do so.

Soon the time came for Sydney to make his trip back to Anchorage, where he was Alaska's foremost painter of land and seascapes. He was also considered the world's greatest painter. But more about that later.

As he was leaving for Alaska, Sydney said, "I will be back next September to get more of your good cooking." It was a rather lonely summer as by that time we realized that we cared a great deal for each other.

On his way to Anchorage he stopped at Juneau to see some friends, Bob and Belle Simpson. When Belle saw him she said, "My goodness, Sydney, you look great. What have you been doing?" He then told her about the French girl that he had been having his dinners with and what an excellent cook she was. He stopped to see them again on his return trip and Belle said, "I bet you are looking forward to seeing your little French girl." "Yes," he replied, "I can hardly wait."

"I am coming to Los Angeles this winter and will come and see you as I would like to meet this girl." She kept her word and one day Sydney came to my studio and told me that a friend of his from Juneau was visiting him and said, "May I invite her to dinner?" "By all means, your friends are my friends."

When Belle came he introduced her to me and we were instantly attracted to each other as ducks to water. After dinner she came to me and said, "Jeanne, why don't you marry the man?" I looked at her and said, "In my country a man has to ask the girl." "Would you marry him if he asked you?" "Yes, provided he did the asking." Back to Sydney she went saying, "Sydney, why don't you marry Jeanne? Did you know that there is someone else after her?" "Oh no! I don't want to lose Jeanne but I would not have the nerve to ask her; she is so much younger than I and looks even younger than she is." "Do not worry about that," she replied, "just don't let her slide away from you."

Again, Belle hurried back to me and said, "Are you sure you would marry Sydney if he asked you?" "Certainly." I promised his doctor that I would look after him the rest of his life. Were we married I could take care of him always.

When Belle left for Juneau, we drove her to the railway station; she kissed us goodbye and said, "When I get back to Juneau I will tell your friends that you will be coming in May, bringing your young bride with you." Sydney turned to me saying, "Did you hear that, Jeanne?" "Yes. I did and it is all right with me."

About three weeks later there came a newspaper from Juneau with an article saying that Sydney Laurence would be coming with his new bride in May. He came to my studio very excited and said, "Read this and tell me when it is going to happen." Like a bolt out of the blue I said, "On the eighth of May" and it was on that date we were married.

Sydney's life was a very colorful and adventurous one. He was born in Brooklyn, New York on October 14th, 1868, of English extraction. His father, Sir Lester Laurence II, was born in Sydney, Australia. His grandfather, Sir Lester Laurence I, was the first governor of Australia when what is now the city of Sydney was known as Botany Bay. Sydney's father was the founder of the insurance company which is now known as the New York Life.

A born artist, Sydney showed his talent as early as the age of nine. One day Sir Lester Laurence went to visit a great friend of his, Edward Moran, who was a very famous painter of marine scenes. During their conversation, he asked the master if he would give lessons to his son, who at the age of nine already showed a great knowledge and skill in painting. "No!" said he, "I do not teach and would not be interested in doing so." The father said no more on the subject and left. The next time he went to visit Edward Moran he took some of Sydney's paintings to show what his youngster could do. "How old did you say the boy is?" "Nine years," said the father. "Remarkable! I have never taught but bring the boy and I will take him under my wing. There is a great talent in the little fellow."

Sydney received his schooling at Peekskill Military Academy, New York.

At the age of seventeen he asked his father if he could join the crew of a boat which toured the world, so he could study the sea, for the purpose of gaining more knowledge of the ocean to paint better marine scenes. This his father refused. Not willing to give up, Sydney stowed away on the brigantine, *Edmond Yates*. When the boat was well under way he climbed out of his hiding place, found the captain and said, "Aye aye, Sir, I am hungry.

Sydney Laurence in a field of Jeanne's wildflowers.

Have you some work for me to do?" The captain looked at the boy and recognized him as the son of his good friend Sir Lester Laurence, who at the time was Commodore of the Yacht Club. "What on earth are you doing on my ship and how did you get on?" "I want to be a seafaring man and I had to stow away as my father would not give me the permission to be one." "You had better get off the ship," said the captain. "The water is too deep and it is too far to swim ashore so you will jolly well keep me on."

Liking the spunk of the boy, the captain sent a courier back to New York to let Sir Lester know that his son was on his ship and to ask what he should do with him. The message came back. "Keep him on board ship for four years, don't let him on shore and make a seafaring man out of him."

Sydney stayed on and traveled all over the world. Eventually he became first mate. The fourth year and his last trip on the *Edmond Yates* ended in a catastrophe. They were returning to England when their ship hit the tail end of a hurricane, which split the boat in two. The mast came down and broke both legs of the captain. Luckily the ship carried lumber which kept it afloat. The order came, "Quick men, wire the ship together the best you can." After doing so, they put splints and stilts on the legs of the captain so he could stand up. "Now men," he said, "there is the lifeboat; it is up to you to decide what to do. We may float for a week, a month or more before a boat will see us and pick us up." The men settled for the lifeboat. Only one man said, "I'll be staying with the captain." That was Sydney. As the last man descended to the lifeboat, all of the men shouted, "Come on Laurence, only the captain goes down with his ship." "No," he answered, "I'll stay right here."

Off they went. They had gone less than one half mile when a big wave upset the lifeboat and all the men fell into the water; another big wave rolled in and took them all under. That was the last they saw of the men.

"Now, my boy," said the captain, "what made you so brave as to stay with me?" "Captain, sir," said Sydney, "I am shaking in my boots on this tub but I was sure that the lifeboat could not survive in this angry sea."

Sydney took over the cooking and alternately keeping watch for another ship to sight them. The days dragged on into weeks. Finally, after they drifted

Two views of Sydneys studio, "My wonderful memories of this place are of a far different Alaska than we have today, yet I would not live any place else in preference to Alaska of today," wrote "Rusty" Huerlin when he sent these photos to Jeanne.

five weeks, a freighter sighted them, came to their rescue and towed them to England. The ship was a total loss. The captain and Sydney were two happy people when they felt solid ground under their feet.

Returning to New York, Sydney entered the National Academy of Designs studying figures under Walter Satterley, marine life under Edward Moran and landscapes under Coni Robert Flori.

In 1889, at the age of twenty four, he went to Paris, entering the Ecole des Beaux Arts, where he spent five years.

His summer vacations were spent in different countries, Germany, Austria, Switzerland and Italy, where he studied and sketched constantly to improve his knowledge and technique in painting. Leaving France for England in 1894, he took up residence in a studio in St. Ives and stayed there quite a few years, during which time his painting was interrupted by several trips as a war correspondent. He was quickly recognized for his marine paintings.

Sydney was elected as an active member of the Royal British Artists and also an honorary member of Cheltenham Fine Arts Society. He was knighted by King Edward VII. He was installed as Mason by the Prince of Wales who was one of his good friends. They often played golf and spent lots of time together.

Sydney was not only master of the brush, he was also a gifted musician, playing the violin, piano, flute and harp. One day while sitting at his studio window, playing his golden harp, a passerby stopped to listen to his playing for quite a while. Finally, he approached the house and rang the doorbell. Sydney opened the door and asked the man, "What can I do for you?" "I want to buy your harp," said the man. "I'll give you four hundred pounds for it; one hundred pounds right now and each year at this time for the next three years I'll bring you one hundred pounds." "I am sorry but the harp is not for sale," said Sydney. "I want that harp; I am a gypsy and we gypsies have a way of getting things. You had better let me have it by tomorrow or your harp will be gone. We will enter your house during the night and you will not hear or see us. We will be out of the house so quietly, harp and all."

After more discussion Sydney decided to let him have it before they stole more than the harp. The man thanked Sydney, gave him the one hundred pounds, and took the harp saying, "I'll be seeing you next year." He then went merrily on his way. Sydney thought that would be the last that he would see of this gypsy. But no, the man kept his word and for the next three years, at about the same time of the year, he showed up bringing the money. "Well, there is honor among gypsies after all," said Sydney.

In the meantime, war broke out with the Zulus. In 1894 Sydney, always looking for adventure, applied for a job as war correspondent with the Black and White Illustration of London, as I recall the name, and was hired.

In this way he was wounded and lost his hearing. While standing with the high officials in the British Square, watching the outcome of the battle, a row of soldiers with fixed bayonets formed a square to restrain the enemy from entering. Disregarding the bayonets, the Zulus climbed over the soldiers and attacked. One of them, swinging his knob-kerry, beat Sydney over the head, destroying an eardrum, which affected his hearing seriously. He was sent back to England to recuperate.

After his recovery he was called as war correspondent to cover the Spanish American War in 1898, which lasted only three months.

In 1899 he was again called as war correspondent by the Black and White Illustration of London to cover the Boer War in South Africa. In this war he was wounded twice. While crossing a bridge on horseback, his horse was shot from under him, taking a piece of flesh out of his buttocks. He scrambled to his feet and ran between all the forces to the other side of the bridge. After he was patched up he asked the doctor to let him go so he could follow his troops. "O.K.," said the doctor, "give this man a horse and let him go on his way." Sydney was barely out two miles when lo and behold his horse was again shot from under him. This time also taking a big hunk out of his posterior. Back to the hospital they took him. The same doctor who took care of him before looked Sydney over and said, "Are you not the same fellow that I took care of just a while ago?" "Yes, that's me." After taking care of his wound the doctor turned to the nurse and said, "Stick this man in the hospital before he comes back with his whole ass shot off."

On his way back to England, Sydney again ran into bad luck. The boat ran into dense fog about seven miles from shore. It was night and everyone was in bed. Suddenly there was a terrific crash as another boat rammed the belly of the ship. "Quick, everybody off," was the order. "We don't know how badly our boat is damaged nor how long we can keep afloat." After taking everyone off and putting them safely on the other vessel, it backed out of the hull of the damaged boat. No sooner had they freed themselves, when the disabled boat sank to the bottom. It was a very hot night and no one had a stitch of clothes on. Sydney grabbed his hat and cane and that is how they marched them back into Cape Town, Africa.

In this caper, Sydney lost everything including the sketches he had ready and the story he had written to deliver to the Black and White Illustration of London. After arriving home he had to do all the sketches and writing from memory.

The following Easter he decided to make a sketching trip on the Mediterranean Sea. One day during the cruise the captain called Sydney on deck and asked him to look at the sunset and tell him what he could see. Sydney

The Art Gallery of the Nugget in Juneau displaying a number of Sydney's paintings. The Proprietor at that time (the early 20's) was Belle G. Simpson.

20

looked and said, "I can see a crucifix with Jesus on the cross in the sunset." The captain replied that he wanted to be sure he was seeing right. Many others looked and also saw the same thing. Looking over the beautiful pastels of the Mediterranean, Sydney called, "Captain, come here. I think I can see a boat in the distance in distress." After looking, the captain replied, "Yes, you are right. We had better go to their assistance fast."

When they got close they saw a scorched lifeboat with just a skeleton of a man standing in it with nine dead bodies around him. The man's tongue was so swollen and protruding out of his mouth that it prevented him from talking. They took him on board the ship and cared for him. After a good rest, they gave him pencil and paper to write down what had happened. His story read that he was the sole survivor of a fishing boat which burned at sea. They barely had time to save the lifeboat and escape. There were many men in the lifeboat but with the terrific heat during the day and without food or water the men could not hold out too long and one by one they died. They buried the first men to die at sea. Later, as they saw many sharks surrounding the boat, they became worried and decided to keep the bodies on board, so as not to make the boat too light. "Days went by and we saw many ships but they did not see us."

The man continued, "Today, the ninth day, being left all alone, while watching the beautiful sunset, I could not believe what I saw; Jesus on the cross in the middle of the sunset. When I saw this miracle in the sky it gave me a ray of hope and I prayed very hard and asked God to send help as I knew I could not hold out much longer. Looking over the pale waters of the Mediterranean I saw a ship in the distance and I hoped and prayed that they would see me. You did and came to my rescue for which I will thank God for the rest of my life."

Sydney was inspired to make a painting of the man in the lifeboat and what he saw in the sky. He told the man (who was an English count) of his plan and asked him if he would come with him to his studio in St. Ives. The count readily consented. From this idea there came to life a large five by seven foot canvas, which he called "The Sole Survivor."

Many of Sydney's sketching trips were made on a bicycle, of which he owned three. To house them he built a shed out of some canvases; paintings he did not like too much. There is a story connected with the bicycle shed.

Coming back from the Spanish American War in 1898, Sydney found an invitation to exhibit a painting at the Paris Salon. Having nothing suitable for exhibition on hand and wanting very much to have a painting at the Paris Salon, Sydney thought about the bicycle shed and all the paintings he used to build it. He took down the roof of the shed, looked it over and took it to his studio, cleaned the painting and worked it over. After he had finished it he sent it to the Paris Salon. He called the painting "Setting Sun, Coast of Cornwall."

During the exhibition, Sydney went to Paris to see the show. Just as he entered the Paris Salon, one of his colleagues, one Ernest Shaw walked out. After greeting him, Sydney asked, "What's the show like?" "Fair," said Ernest, "but there is one outstanding painting which struck me as the best. It received the 'Hors de Concours' which means 'Beyond Competition.'" "Tell me what the subject is and who the painter is," asked Sydney.

"I do not know who the painter is nor the title of the painting but the subject is a seascape with a sunset so well painted that it dazzles your eyes." "That sounds like my painting," Sydney replied. "Now I have to go back in and find out if it is your painting or not." It was.

After the exhibition was over the French Government bought it for twenty five thousand francs, to be hung in the Luxembourg Gallery in Paris.

Previous to this exhibition, Sydney had some paintings exhibited in the Paris Salon. One in 1896 received a third class medal. For another in 1897 he was awarded a second class medal. It is interesting to know that in those days the first class medals went to portraits and still life only.

The fourth and last war Sydney was called on by the Black and White Illustration was in 1900. It was the Boxer Rebellion in China, which lasted only three months. Again Sydney had an unusual and funny experience.

After a long hard walk the troops halted for a rest in a railroad yard. Being dead tired, Sydney climbed into a freight car and was soon sound asleep.

How long he slept he never knew. Getting out of the freight car and much to his surprise, he was staring at strange yellow faces, those of the Boxers. He asked, "Where is my troop and what happened during my peaceful sleep?" One Boxer, an Oxford graduate, stepped forward saying, "As of now, you are a prisoner of the Boxers. The English are on the run."

"Oh, no. You've got to let me go; I am a war correspondent and not a soldier. I have to follow my troops and report what is going on."

After translating what Sydney had said to him, they held a conference and decided that he looked like a harmless little fellow. They asked for his credentials and after checking them they said, "You may go." At first he thought that he had not heard right but suddenly realizing they meant it, he thanked them and turned on the run, expecting to be shot at any minute, but nothing happened. Eventually he found and joined the British troops again.

Returning to England, he made a few sketching trips, painting around Kent, Cambridge and finally settling in Ramsgate.

In 1901 Queen Victoria died and Sydney was commissioned to paint her as she lay in state. He had only three days in which to do the painting and he needed a rather large canvas. Not having one on hand, he looked around his studio at his paintings and noticing the "Sole Survivor" he looked at it and said, "You will do." This painting, being mostly in pastels, lent itself very nicely to the subject. He always had a small study of the subjects he painted and later on he painted the "Sole Survivor" on another large canvas. This is now owned by a Mr. Lloyd Martin of Honolulu, Hawaii.

Hearing much talk about the Klondike in Alaska, he returned to New York where he visited his mother. At this time he also visited with his artist friends at the luxurious Salmagundi Artist's Club of New York, of which he was a member.

Knowing that Alaska was a very cold place, he outfitted himself with warm clothes, including a raccoon coat and hat. Now he was ready for the trip to the great unknown. Little did he know of all the hardships awaiting him. Starting this journey, he took the train to Seattle, Washington and from there the boat to Alaska. This was in 1904.

In Seattle people began to discourage Sydney saying, "By now you are a little too late for the Klondike. Most of the land is staked out and explored. You won't have much of a chance there anymore. If you are wise you will stay right here and stake out a claim and work it. There is lots of money to be made right here."

But he was determined to go on. On arriving at Tyonek he met a few prospectors returning from the Klondike, tired, worn and empty handed. They also advised him not to go on. Arriving in Juneau, where the boat stopped over, he found some prospectors who had struck it rich. They encouraged him to stay saying, "There are a lot of places in Alaska where gold can be found. Our advice to you is to stay and try your luck right here."

Since he was getting low on cash he decided to stay in Juneau for a while, where he took a job as photographer.

When spring came Sydney's restless and adventurous nature did not let him rest until he was on a boat again. This time he landed in Valdez. Looking the little city over and wondering what his next move would be, he saw a building going up for a saloon. He stopped to watch the men at work. The foreman saw him standing there and went over to him and said, "Are you a carpenter?" "Yes, I am," Sydney replied. "Go get your tools and overalls and get busy." Thinking quickly, Sydney said, "I am sorry but all my belongings are at the bottom of the ocean. My boat capsized and everything went with it."

Turning to the workmen the foreman said, "Give this fellow some tools and overalls and put him to work."

It was lunch time and all the men went to lunch. The foreman told him to put up a door during the time they were gone. It was a beautiful mahogany door to the entrance of the saloon. Taking the door to the opening he found it was too high, not noticing a board which had to be removed to fit the door in place. He measured the height of the space and shaved the door off to fit it and had the door in place when the men came from lunch. The foreman noticed the mistake immediately and turned to Sydney and said, "How long have you been a carpenter?" "As of now," was the answer. The foreman shook his head and said, "It would not be a bad job had you first removed the board; the door would have fit perfectly." Never the less, he kept him on as he needed men so badly and he worked there until the completion of the saloon.

During the following seven years Sydney forgot his paint and brushes and went prospecting during the summer months and worked on all kinds of jobs during the winter. Some of them as carpenter, cook, lumber jack, a licensed boat pilot, storekeeper, photographer and so on.

With the spring breakup, the urge for prospecting became so great that again he would be off for the hills, seeking the illusive pot of gold. When asked what drove him to it he would quote Robert W. Service's poem.

> "For once you've panned the speckled sand
>   And seen the bonny dust
> Its peerless brightness blinds you
>   And you go because you must."

He always found enough gold to get him started for the winter. The second winter he spent in Cordova. One day while he was standing at the dock watching people get on the boat, which was ready to sail for Seattle, a restaurant owner came running and, when he saw Sydney, called out, "Hey Laurence, can you cook?" "I can fix ham and eggs, beans, potatoes, steaks, stews and a few other things." "Good. Here are the keys to the restaurant. Take over until I get back; I've just received a wire that my mother is very ill. I'll be back as soon as I can." Before Sydney could say no, the man was up the plank and on the boat. That is how he became a cook for a while.

The next boat from Seattle brought some tourists in the early morning hours. One traveling salesman came into the restaurant and ordered a Spanish omelet. He had no idea of how to make one but did not want the man to know so he went to the kitchen, pretending he was not alone, and called out, "One Spanish omelet." Soon he came out of the kitchen saying, "I am sorry but the cook said that he is all out of Spanish omelets but we have ham and eggs." The stranger started to laugh and said, "Get in that kitchen and fix me ham and eggs. I know that you are alone. I am a friend of the owner and come here about every three months."

With summer on its way, Sydney bought himself a boat. He left Cordova and sailed to Tyonek on Cook Inlet. From there he started out ever searching for the illusive gold.

Returning in the autumn to Tyonek he got a job as boat pilot, picking up people from different canneries, of which there were quite a few along the coast. Fishing was one of Alaska's largest industries but during the winter the canneries closed and their workers and owners left for Seattle. He also took homesteaders and miners up Cook Inlet to their various places. At that time there was not an Anchorage. There were only a few homesteaders and the ranger, Jack Brown and his wife, Nellie. Jack and Nellie became very good friends of Sydney's.

Finally Sydney could no longer resist the strong desire to paint again. He bought some water colors, brushes and a sketch book and carried them with him wherever he went. With all the beauty of this great land it was not hard to find interesting subjects to paint. From his brushes came many sunsets, sunrises, seascapes, caches or whatever scene struck his fancy, and he accumulated quite an assortment of paintings.

In 1912 when Mt. Katmai blew its top, Sydney and another man were prospecting about fifty miles from the mountain. They had just finished staking a claim where they had found gold and were ready to leave and go register their find. Both of them had filled a poke of gold. Each poke held about $3000.00 worth. Suddenly they heard a big rumble, which so often precedes an avalanche. Soon the air was filled with ashes, breathing was difficult and their skin became irritated and stung sharply. Only then did they realize that a volcano had erupted. The ash fell all around them until it was over a foot deep, destroying all vegetation. The acid in the air was so strong that it ate up their tent, clothing and the pokes of gold. Everything crumbled to ashes, leaving them stripped naked with very red and inflamed bodies. The wild life also disappeared. In this condition they had to flee, hiking about thirty miles to find a prospector who gave them shelter and lent them overalls.

... *by* *JEANNE LAURENCE*

After a good night's rest they went on their way again heading for a trading post about twenty miles away. When they arrived there they bought clothing and other things they needed, which they arranged to pay for later.

Sydney decided to stay along Cook Inlet for the rest of the summer and fall, working the sand for gold. His partner decided to move on. By November, when the ground had frozen too hard to work it, he loaded his belongings and the little gold he had found into his open dory and started the journey down Cooks Inlet to spend the winter in Valdez. Unexpectedly, a stiff northwesterly wind started blowing. Being about five miles from shore, he turned toward land for safety. Toward evening the wind became much stronger and the waves became dangerously large. Knowing he could not survive the storm, he made for shore for a landing, heading to where he knew a cannery was located. Although he knew it would be closed for the winter, trappers and prospectors felt privileged to use these canneries at any time, especially in time of need. Approaching the shore, he wondered how he could climb the embankment. He decided to wait for a lull in the breakers which came every so often; at the opportune moment he backed into the shore and jumped out. The next wave seemed to be breaking above him, mountainously high. He turned to scramble up the frozen and slippery beach

Sydney in his Los Angeles Studio at 1719 Clinton Street taken in the late 20's or early 30's. This studio was maintained for seven years.

when a wave caught him, knocking him down and rolling him over and over. He slipped back with the receding water face downward, legs spread apart; he tried to dig a hole with his fingers and his boots. Before the next wave broke he managed to get his feet up on the beach. Looking back he saw his boat split in half and his belongings swirling in the foamy water. Everything he had aboard, including the little gold, was lost. It was a disaster.

He was stunned from the beating of the water upon him against the frozen beach. He set out for the cannery building trying to run but his freezing clothes prevented free movement. It was some time before he located the building. It was getting dark and he felt the cold bitterly.

It was the Alaskan custom for each person leaving the place to lay a fire for the next arrival. Sydney found the fire prepared but there were no matches. Fumbling awkwardly for his match box, which was a strong metal container with a screwed-on top, he found it only to discover that by some unfortunate means the match box had opened and was drenched with water and of no use. Abandoning all hope for a fire he sat down saying, "Well, Laurence, this is the end for you."

Not liking the idea of just sitting there to freeze to death, he began thinking hard of what he should do next. Then he remembered an Indian village quite some miles away. "I'd better try for it," he thought, "instead of just sitting here to freeze."

There were two rivers about thirty feet wide to be crossed. Into the first one he waded and swam across. The swiftness of the water prevented it from freezing. The water felt welcomingly warm against his body. Nevertheless, the additional wetting of his clothes caused more ice to form on him. Clumsily he moved on. In addition to the hampering effect of his frozen clothes, he was troubled with the loss of feeling.

He swam the second stream, heading into the wooded territory toward the Indian village. He was forced to grope along being cautious to keep his balance for there was no way for him to get back on his feet again once he fell down. He had lost practically all control of his frozen feet and legs and swung them along like pendulums.

His mind was alert for the sound of dogs barking. He knew when he heard the howl of the malamutes that the Indians would know there was someone out there and they would come looking. It was none too soon as he could not have gone one step farther. He fell and they picked him up and took him inside and cared for him. By now his legs, feet, arms and hands were frozen solid. To defrost his frozen limbs the kind Indians bathed them and made compresses out of coal oil. Snow or water was not used. The pain of thawing his limbs out was excruciating. As luck would have it, the marrow of the bones was not frozen. The members were swollen to twice their size and resembled the color of red beets. For days the storm kept raging and day and night the Indians cared for Sydney.

The Indians lived in houses quite unlike a white man's. A hole in the roof provided entrance and exit. Heat came from a fire on the floor inside. A ladder gave access to the roof opening. In this way prowling animals were kept out. The Indians were possessed with an invariable friendliness. Through the kindness and help they gave Sydney, his life was saved.

Finally the storm subsided and they put him on a dog sled and took him down the coast to Seldovia. From there he was carried by steamer to Valdez where he was hospitalized. The doctor came and looked Sydney over and when he saw his legs he said, "I am sorry but we have to amputate these legs." Sydney looked at the doctor and said, "Doctor, these legs go with this little fellow and the little fellow goes with these legs so you jolly well leave them alone." "You are a spunky little devil but sooner or later we will have to amputate them when gangrene sets in." "Then we will wait until then," Sydney replied.

Through November and December his convalescence was tediously slow. His feet and hands improved and by the end of December he was walking on crutches.

On Christmas eve he asked the nurse if he could go out for a while. "No," she said, "You are only going to get drunk." "First of all, I am not a drinking man," said Sydney, "and second, I have no money to buy a drink with." "All right, you may go for a little while but don't forget to come back," said the nurse.

His movements were still uncertain and painful. He made his way to the Seattle Saloon in Valdez where he found a gay and colorful crowd. Some of his friends saw him come in and called, "Hey, Laurence, come over here, join us and have a drink." "I have not a bean to my name. All my possessions are down in the ocean." "Never mind," they said, "we will treat you." Sydney sat down with the group and watched them playing cards.

Valdez was a beautiful spot, situated on the ocean and surrounded by majestic mountains. From time to time, Sydney looked out the window watching the glorious sunset when suddenly an inspiration struck him. Turning to his friends he said, "Boys, look at this beautiful sunset," and in a sentimental mood he added, "I wonder why no artist has ever gone to Mount McKinley to paint. That would be a great challenge for any artist and a wonderful piece of work could be painted."

"Now who would risk their life to make a journey so far and treacherous?" they said. "I would," he replied. They looked at him like he had lost all of his marbles. "We will bet that you cannot even hold a brush," said one of the men.

"Yes, I can swing a brush." Sydney was feeling good and in a boastful way let them know of all the honors he had received. He told them about the painting that the French government had bought for the Louvre in Paris; also, that he belonged to the Royal British Artists, the Cheltenham Art Society in London, England and that he was a member of the Salmagundi Artist Club of New York.

In astonishment they looked at him, wondering if it really could be so and if it was true.

"Now when you boys are willing to grubstake me, I will make the trip to Mount McKinley and paint you a ten thousand dollar painting."

Before he knew what was happening, one of the men took off his hat and emptied his pockets saying, "Let's see if we can get a grubstake together for Laurence."

All told they got four hundred dollars together. There were five in the party. Besides that, they gave Sydney a letter of credit for whatever he would need for the trip. They realized he needed more than four hundred dollars as it is a year's job to get in to Mount McKinley and come out again.

Sydney just had enough sense left to hasten out of that saloon before they changed their minds. He never knew how he got to the dock where a boat was leaving that night for Seward. He did not stop to buy a ticket. He stumbled along on those crutches until he found the smoking room and sat there. It seemed that the boat would never start. All the time he was afraid the men would be coming to get their money back. Finally the boat was on its way. He went to the purser and asked for a ticket to Seward. "How did you get on the boat without being seen?" "Never mind, I am here and now I want to pay for my fare."

Arriving at Seward, Sydney got off the boat and sent an order to Seattle for paints, brushes and all the other materials he needed for his work. He did not wait for the order to come from Seattle; it would have taken too long and he was anxious to start the journey to Mount McKinley. He bought five dogs, a sled and the essentials he needed for the trip.

Now, it was the dead of winter. Still on crutches, he began the four hundred mile hike to Mount McKinley. His feet and hands were extremely sensitive to the cold. He had a job to do and he stubbornly trudged on. After the first two hundred miles, over a narrow trail, he arrived in Susitna. There he bought the rest of his needs.

Now the actual work began as there was no trail to follow. It seems inconceivable that Sydney, in his weakened convalescing condition, would start on such a dangerous and difficult expedition. The men who had grubstaked him realized the serious hazards very clearly and little expected to hear from or see Sydney again.

Traveling as he did was a laborious process. All the way into the Mount McKinley region it was necessary for him to go on ahead of the dogs on snow shoes and pack down a trail. After this the dogs could travel over the trail without falling through and wallowing in the snow. Going over the trail with the sled packed it down harder. There were also relay trips to be made. It was impossible to haul everything at one time on the sled. Seven relay trips were required to move the supplies and equipment. Each day Sydney and his dogs made about forty miles back and forth.

The caches were made by placing spruce saplings on the snow and loading them with the luggage. The whole pile then was covered with a sled tarpaulin and boughs as protection against the wolves.

Day in and day out his hauling and trail work went on. Evenings, on the return trip, the dogs were fed. They knew it and came in flying with tails up; whereas, in the morning they walked to the harness without much enthusiasm, their tails carried low.

It took March, April and May to reach Mount McKinley. He pitched his tent on the southern side, about forty five miles from the top, at the edge of the timber line, on a knoll where there were a few spruce trees growing. From there he had a beautiful outlook of the mountain overlooking a valley. Three glaciers could be seen at the foot of Mount McKinley. They formed a river called Tokasheetna. Tokasheetna comes from Indian and Russian; "Toka" means three, "sheet" meaning ice and "na" meaning water. Together they mean "three icy waters,"

Before he could start painting he had to make one more trip in to Seward to pick up his supplies which he had ordered from Seattle and which were being held for him in Seward. It only took a few days to make the trip to Seward as it was mostly downhill; whereas, it had taken him months coming in. The return trip took somewhat longer.

Now back in camp and before he could get to the project of painting, more work had to be done. Firewood had to be hauled from quite a distance. Using the dogs and sled he made a number of trips. Enough wood was gathered for the summer months. The next thing he needed was an easel which he built out of his sled. With the easel finished and set up he was ready to go to work.

He would sit in front of his tent studying Mount McKinley in its different moods. The soft morning light, the changes of color during the day, the evening sunset with its rose colored glow on the mountain; each was a breathtaking sight. As he contemplated all this indescribable beauty a tenseness crept over him and he was filled with fear that he might not be able to do justice to it. Setting up his palette and starting on his first study the first attempt went awkwardly but he kept on plugging away and before long he was in the swing of it and his doubts left him. Most of the summer was spent around Mount McKinley studying and painting it in its various moods. By fall he had forty five studies ready.

Having used his sled for an easel, he decided to leave before winter set in. Now the heavy chore began. All of his possessions had to be carried down to the flats on his back to the Tokasheetna River. There he joined some miners and prospectors who also were ready to make the trip down the river. His dogs he gave to a miner who was remaining for the winter. The oak easel he left standing on the exact spot where he used it. He left everything behind that he could do without.

When they started there were ten men on the boat, eleven dogs, and the camping equipment of each man. The boat was filled to capacity. They camped on it and cooked all their meals all the way down. When they came to the rapids a German started to stand up and all of the men yelled, "Sit down; you cannot take it standing up." Before they were through telling him, they struck a rock and upside down in the boat he went. There he lay, head down and legs up. No one could help him as all of them had to hang on for dear life. It is a very ticklish affair to run the rapids. Finally they came to the end of them. As they helped the man up, he looked at everyone, shook his head and said in his droll German, "I have been through them rapids and through them rapids and have not seen 'em yet."

The trip down the Tokasheetna and Susitna Rivers brought Sydney to Susitna where a motor launch took him to Hope farther down the river. From there he made the trip over the mountains in relay trips to Seward. Everything had to be carried on his back. Eventually he got passage on a steamer to Valdez. After arriving at Valdez he looked around for a suitable studio, where he could paint the large canvas he had promised his friends. After finding what he was looking for, he settled down to begin the enormous task of painting Mount McKinley.

Almost a year had passed since he had left Valdez. Now, December of 1913, his return caused some consternation. The story had gotten started that he had frozen to death on the trail. They were definite in the identification of the body found on the trail. All those who had grubstaked him felt deeply the guilt of sending him to Mount McKinley in the condition he was in. The thought that they had sent him on such a project weighed heavily upon them and would be a constant source of regret.

Wondering if he could find some of the men who had grubstaked him, Sydney walked down the street to the Seattle Saloon. Sure enough, there he found two of his friends. When they saw him they jumped up saying, "Stay away from us. We just knew that some day your ghost would come and haunt us."

"Hey, stand still. I may look like a ghost but I am flesh and blood and very much alive but I'll admit looking wild and wooly with my beard." He added, "Now tell me about the ghost you think I am."

Finally they collected their wits and said, "Last winter a prospector came back from his mine maintaining that he found Laurence's frozen body on the trail."

"Well, that was not me because here I am back and ready to paint the promised picture for you."

The painting of Mount McKinley, a six foot by twelve foot picture, was done from sketches he brought back with him. He wanted to do an appealing painting of this picturesque mountain. He succeeded. Not only did he paint an appealing one but also a very famous one, an unforgettable tribute to Mount McKinley.

After it was finished there arose the question, what to do with it. They put their heads together and decided to send it, as a loan, to the Art Gallery at the Museum in Washington, D.C. This they did where it hung for many years. After Sydney's death the painting was moved to the Smithsonian Institution in Washington, D. C.

With the large painting delivered and his sketches sold, he readied himself for another trip to Mount McKinley to paint more studies of the mountain. This was in November of 1914.

He started on this trip with only three dogs. The lead dog and two dogs harnessed to the sled. He made the trip in due time finding his old camp and everything he had left intact. He erected his tent and stocked firewood. Now he was ready to paint. Many beautiful winter scenes came from his brushes, also spring scenes and a few summer ones.

This particular winter was a hard and very cold one. Getting low on firewood, Sydney decided one morning to go down hill and fetch some. It was an especially cold morning and the dogs did not want to go. When he started to hitch them to the sled they pulled back. Finally he had them harnessed and with a big "Mush on!" they were on their way. Mushing on he started to feel cold and his legs became numb. He thought, "Now I know why the dogs did not want to go. It must be well under zero." "Well, boys, you tried to tell me. We better turn back." With that he unhitched the dogs and they turned and ran as fast as they could back to camp. Leaving the sled behind, Sydney also headed back for the warmth of his tent.

This experience caused him to catch a cold which turned into pneumonia. Getting sicker and sicker and with a high fever, he thought, "This is the end of me." With this thought in mind he sat down and wrote a note saying who he was and what should be done with his belongings and his remains. He pinned the note to his sleeping bag. He fed the dogs well and unleashed them from their chains so they could run free. Stoking the fire to capacity, he then climbed into his sleeping bag, closed it up tight and went to sleep with the firm belief that he would never wake up again.

How long he lay there he never knew. Eventually he awoke feeling very hungry and weak. He could not understand why he felt as he did but collecting his wits it suddenly came to him that he had been very sick with pneumonia and had not expected to ever come out of it. He then thought of the dogs. What had become of them? They must be very hungry by now. To his surprise, when he opened the sleeping bag, he found all three of them lying around him and keeping him warm. This most likely had saved his life.

When he got out of the bag and on his feet he felt weak and very wobbly but he made a fire and warmed food for the dogs as they looked very starved.

After the dogs were well fed he thought of himself and fixed and ate a good meal.

Recuperating slowly, he resumed his work again. With spring gone and summer starting, Sydney made plans to leave Mount McKinley in mid-summer and not be caught in the cold winter again. Fixing his sled with four little wheels, he loaded up and off he went with equipment, sled and dogs. This time he stopped at Anchorage. Plans were in the making to build a railroad between Seward and Fairbanks.

At this time there were but a few families in Anchorage. Sydney found a little cabin which was situated near the spot where they intended to build the railroad. He moved in.

An official of the railroad, passing his cabin, saw him and asked, "What are you doing this winter, old-timer?" "Nothing in particular," was his answer. "All right then, cut some railroad ties for us and earn a few dollars." Sydney did just that and by spring he had about three hundred ready for them.

Now in the spring of 1915 he again prepared to make one more trip in to Mount McKinley. A nostalgic yearning had come over him for the mountain which intrigued him so much. He felt that he still had to see much more of its charm and beauty. This time he hired two Indians to help him carry his belongings and provisions in to Mount McKinley.

All went well as long as the mountain was not in view but at the first sight of it the Indians put down their packs saying, "This is as far as we go." "What is this all about?" asked Sydney. "You were hired to get me all the way to Mount McKinley." "The big eagle lives there and big eagle eats bad Indians and we are bad Indians." Nothing could persuade them to go on and they left him stranded. Luckily it was not too many miles to the old camp.

After three months of studying and painting around Mount McKinley Sydney prepared for the return trip to Anchorge. He had to carry all of his belongings in relay trips, having been alone in camp. His gold pan, pick and shovel were always with him as he prospected all along the way.

One evening, after he had set up his camp for the night, he went in search of gold. This time he was lucky enough to find a spot that seemed fairly rich. He staked out a claim and recorded it on his return trip to Anchorage.

He looked for a partner to work the claim and found one of his miner friends who was willing to go and work the grounds. They named the place "Poor Man's Creek." Every summer for years Monroe Cast worked the ground, taking out quite a nice amount of gold; however, they never found the mother lode.

On his return to Anchorage he found it flourishing with many houses, schools and businesses being constructed. The building of the railroad had progressed and Anchorage was chosen as an ideal spot for its headquarters.

Sydney was at a loss to know what to do during the winter to keep busy. Being a camera lover and a good photographer the thought struck him to open a camera shop and that is what he did. This also gave him the opportunity to display his water color paintings.

With the completion of the railroad, tourists began flocking to the interior of Alaska to see its beauty for themselves. They found that Alaska was not all ice and snow like most everyone thought. One day, a tourist, a high official from Washington, D. C. came into the photo shop with a roll of films and said, "I would like to have these films developed right away." "That will take time," said Sydney. "I know that but I have time to wait," he replied. "Make yourself at home and look around," and with that Sydney disappeared into the dark room.

Noticing some paintings on the wall the man studied them wondering who the artist was who had so expertly painted them. When Sydney returned from the dark room the stranger asked who had painted the water colors. "I did," was his reply. "What are you doing behind that counter? When a man can turn out paintings like these he should stay with it. What are you asking for them?" Sydney figured out the amount and told him the price of the lot. Without saying a word, the man took out his check book and wrote a check for the amount mentioned and handed it to him. At the same time he gave him instructions to send them to his address in Washington, D. C.

After the customer had departed Sydney began to wonder if he were in the wrong business and if he should devote all of his time to painting.

With Anchorage growing the city was in need of a hotel. A Mr. and Mrs. Frank Reed decided to build an apartment hotel. Sydney gave up his photo shop and rented an apartment from the Reeds and opened a studio devoting his entire time to painting.

The Reeds became very close friends of his and when tourists and visitors were in town Pauline Reed took them to his studio and very often sold paintings for him. One day Pauline expressed the thought that she would like to have a large painting of Mount McKinley for the parlor but could not afford to pay the price of such a painting. "That can be arranged," said Sydney. "I'll tell you what I'll do; you pay for the material and let me have one year's rent free and you will have a painting." "It would be wonderful if you would do that," said Pauline.

A six by twelve canvas was stretched and the work began. This particular painting was done right in the parlor of the hotel where it remained until the deaths of Mr. and Mrs. Reed. It was a great attraction for the hotel. Visitors and tourists from all over the U.S.A. never missed stopping at the hotel to see this magnificient work of art. They could not help wondering how a man could portray the grandeur and splendor of this mountain so well on canvas.

The Reed's two sons, Paul and Frank, inherited the painting. They were very proud of their possession and let the painting travel to different states of the U.S.A. for exhibition. It now hangs on the wall of the Matanuska Valley Bank in Anchorage where everyone has a chance to see it.

In the following years Sydney made many sketching trips during the summer. Many times he visited with Monroe Cast at the Poor Man's Creek diggings. Working the mine for gold did not appeal to Sydney; there was too much dirt mixed with the gold. What he liked best was to prospect and locate places where gold could be found. During his wanderings, stopping here and there, he found a few places that looked prosperous which he staked and recorded but he never worked them. He would rather let other people do that. One of his claims was worked by Dick Francis and one by a German couple. These particular mines produced a great amount of gold. Sydney never accepted anything in return for letting people work his claims. He said that the man who digs for gold is entitled to all he can get out of the ground.

One day, hiking out from Poor Man's Creek, he encountered two young fellows. They stopped him and asked, "Old timer, could you tell us a place where we could find gold and how to work it?" "I sure can," he replied, "I have a claim and I am not working it. I will lead you to it and you are welcome to all you can take out this summer."

The boys wanted just enough gold to go back to San Francisco to open a business. Sydney told them that they needed picks and shovels and some hose and boards to build a sluice box. He gave them instructions as to how to build it. They followed his advice and during this summer took out fifty thousand dollars worth of gold. They returned to San Francisco and set themselves up in business. Many years later, in 1936, two gentlemen came and paid him a visit at his studio in Anchorage. "We wonder if you remember us?" they asked Sydney. "We are the boys you gave permission to take gold out of your mining claim that we might go into business. We have come to thank you again. Today we are the proud owners of a large department store in San Francisco." "It makes me very happy to know that you were successful in your undertaking," Sydney replied.

Sydney Laurence was a man to help everyone. I dare say that in his entire life he did only good. He was always ready to lend a helping hand and felt very badly when he could not help a friend in need.

Anchorage people often came to visit him in his studio and to admire his works, wishing they could own one of his paintings but did not have the money. He would watch them to find out which of the paintings they liked best, the one they could not take their eyes off of. He would then take it off the wall and hand it to them saying, "Take this home with you. Hang it on your wall and enjoy it." Many could not believe they had heard right and would say, "We just cannot accept such a beautiful and valuable gift."

"Sure you can. You like the painting so much that you should have it," was his reply.

Now came the year of 1926. By September of that year Sydney did not feel too well and his doctor advised him to move to a warmer climate for the winter. He chose Los Angeles, California for a change of scenery. That was the year that I was the lucky girl to meet him.

We were married on the eighth day of May, 1928. Our honeymoon was a trip to Alaska where we spent the summer. We first landed in Ketchikan. We then went to Juneau where we stayed for two months. We had an apartment over the Nugget Shop which our good friends, Robert and Belle Simpson, owned. Sydney rented a car and we went sketching every day. Leaving Juneau for Anchorage by boat we stopped at Seward and stayed for one week. From there we took the train to Anchorage making one stop at Lake Kenai to visit Nellie Lyon's museum. Everyone got off the train to pay a quick visit to Nellie, who was quite a well known character throughout Alaska. She had many interesting artifacts to show at her museum and many stories to tell.

When we arrived in Anchorage we found many friends of Sydney's waiting to greet us. I was very well received; everyone made me welcome. Immediately I felt at home and in love with the country which reminded me of Switzerland. It did not take me long to get acquainted with the beauty and splendor of the surroundings of Anchorage. There was only twenty four miles of road called "the loop road." One entered at one end and emerged at the other. One six mile road leading to Lake Spenard and a four mile road which brought you to Lake Otis.

There are many mountain ranges around Anchorage. One of them is the Chugiak Range and another the Alaska Range, which is snow capped the whole year round. Another is the Susitna Mountain also called the "Sleeping Lady." By studying its outline carefully one can see the form of a woman lying on its top.

The summer went by too fast but with October on the way we began to prepare for the trip back to Los Angeles where we had kept our studios. I hated to leave Anchorage as I had made so many friends that I did not like to leave behind. Sydney, whom I had nicknamed Sweety, was such a wonderful man, full of kindness. He was short of stature, being only five feet seven, and was extremely witty. Since I was so much younger, he called me Kid.

On our way back to California we spent a week in Juneau. We stayed in Seattle for a few days where we bought a car and drove back to Los Angeles. After a long stretch of road Sweety said to me, "Now you take the wheel and drive for a while." I did not say anything but took the wheel and started driving. For a long time it was a straight road and all went well but when I came to a right hand turn I said to myself, "Now watch your step making this turn." You see, I had never driven a car before and I took the corner too sharply and I ran down into the barrow pit but I stepped on the gas and climbed right out of it. "How did you do that and how long have you been driving?" asked Sweety. "As of now," I replied. Sweety said, "When we get to Los Angeles you go and take driving lessons and buy yourself a car."

He did not take the wheel from me, however, but let me go on as there was a long stretch of straight road ahead. I saw in the distance a bridge with a big truck crossing it. "Sweety," I said, "Don't you think you should take the wheel now and do the driving?" After changing seats he saw the big truck coming toward us and he said, "No wonder you asked me to take over. You were scared." I was. After we returned to Los Angeles I bought myself a car and took driving lessons.

One of my close friends came almost every day and picked me up and we went to the beaches where I made sketches. Sydney, who had many orders for paintings, stayed in his studio and painted. One day I said to him, "Sweety, you know I would like to paint Mount McKinley myself." He said, "That is good, Kid, but you will have to hike for it. I did. I do not want you ever to copy anybody for you have it in you to make your own originals. I will take you to my old camp, where I painted and made many sketches, for I also would like to go back and make more studies from the same spot." We were soon making plans for a trip to Alaska in the spring of 1929.

When Sydney mentioned to our neighbor, Arthur Granke, that we were thinking of making a trip in to Mount McKinley for the summer he asked if he could go along as our campman. Sydney thought that would be all right as we needed someone to take care of the camp.

We left Los Angeles early in April of 1929, stopping at Juneau and Anchorage for a while. The first of May we left Anchorage by train to Talkeetna. We had to wait about three weeks for the snow to melt so we could hike over the trail to the camp. For the first fifty eight miles we had a road just wide enough for the wheels of the wagon to go over.

The wagon was loaded very high with all our belongings and food, enough to carry us through the summer and autumn. "Come on, Jeanne, we will put you on top of the wagon." "Oh no," I said, "I will not ride on top of that wagon going over this humpty, dumpty road." Turning to Sydney I said, "Sweety, may I walk?" "Sure you may. We will pick you up along the way. It is twenty four miles to the first stop where we will stay overnight. I am sure you cannot walk that far. You are just scared to sit and ride on the top." And I was.

A Swiss miner who was on his return to his mine said, "I will walk with her." "That will be fine," said Sydney.

Off we went and kept walking until we reached the cabin which belonged to the Road Commission. Anyone coming along the road was welcome to use the cabin, cook their meals and spend the night. From time to time the horses had to be rested and that made us one good half hour ahead of them. While waiting for them we lit the stove and cooked a big pot of spaghetti. We had it ready when they arrived and fixed the steaks they brought along. Sydney could not understand how I walked all those miles and had dinner half cooked before they arrived.

After the dishes were cleared away we prepared for bed. Sweety and I had a big bunk on which we laid our sleeping bags and climbed in for a well earned rest. About four o'clock Sweety poked me in the ribs and said, "Time to get up and cook breakfast."

Not knowing that I had undressed as I cannot sleep with clothes on, he said, "Kid, get up; I want the boys to know what a good cook and wife you are." I opened the sleeping bag and asked, "Should I come out this way?" "Oh no, quick, put your clothes on!"

After dressing, I made a fire in the stove and cooked hot cakes, ham and eggs. The Swiss fellow heard me up and asked, "Have you got to cook breakfast?" "Yes," I answered, "Sydney is so proud of me he wants everybody to know what all I can do." "I will lend you a hand," which he did.

In a camp it is customary to wash the dishes, put the fire out, lay another one and put the cabin in order ready for the next traveler who comes along. After all the work was done, I said to my Swiss friend, "Let's get started ahead of them.

When I told Sweety that we were going to walk again he said, "Go to it, Kid, because today I know you will not walk another twenty four miles to our next stop." We fooled him and were one good hour ahead of them.

This cabin was in a spot near a nice stream with plenty of trout, so many we could almost catch them in our hands. Before the hour was over we had caught forty fish for our dinner.

When they arrived, Sweety shook his head saying, "Kid, you surprise me. I never thought that you were such a good walker." After a nice fish dinner we prepared for bed. There were not enough bunks, so Sydney and I chose a long table on which we laid our sleeping bags.

At five o'clock in the morning I got breakfast, put everything in order and was ready to start, this time on horseback. We had two horses and two mules, the latter being loaded with provisions. Sweety and I rode the horses which were large dray horses. The packer, who also took care of the animals, asked me, "Did you ever ride a horse?" "Yes," I said, "you know the horses you ride in the park, where one pokes the nose up in the air and clacks with the tongue." He laughed and said, "Get on that horse woman; you will never be the same when you get off."

We had ridden about sixteen miles when he asked me, "How goes it?" "Fine," I said, "but I have no feeling. I am numb." Before I knew what had happened he had pulled me off my horse, grabbed a stick and poked me with it saying "Walk, woman, walk!" "I can't. Just let me stop a few minutes." "No, I cannot let you. You've got to walk to get the blood back in circulation, otherwise you will not get on your feet again."

He made me walk until the numbness was completely out of my body. "Now, you are going to walk for three miles. After that you may ride again."

Everyone standing there was laughing. I must have been a funny sight walking like a drunk. I could not keep my feet under me. Three miles farther Sweety was waiting for me with my horse. After another twenty three miles we reached our next stop which was Dick Francis' cabin.

"Here is where we are going to eat. One always finds a pot of beans cooking on the stove for all who pass by and are hungry," said Sydney. "Dick expects them to go in and help themselves." Sure enough, on entering we found a pot of beans cooked and ready to eat.

We were all very hungry and I can say I do not think I ever ate better beans in my life. Dick was not there when we arrived but came soon after we had finished dinner. It was heart warming to see the greetings of the two old friends who had not seen each other for a number of years.

Early next morning we got underway. Dick and his seven huskies joined our group. He wanted to come along and help find Sydney's old camp and to give a hand in putting up the tents. Poor Man's Creek was our next stop, Sydney's old mining camp, which was about twenty six miles from Dick's place.

Sweety and I were getting very stiff from riding and I wondered how I would ever get off the horse. Sweety said, "Come on, Kid, and I will show you. Let's get off before the others get here and see us." With that he rode to a ladder which was leaning against a cache. He stepped on a rung and gave the horse a little pat on his side and it walked away from under him. I then did the same thing. When the others arrived they were surprised to find us off the horses. We did not tell them the method we used.

The next day Arthur, Jeff and Dick started over the mountain to look for Sydney's old camp, leaving us behind. This also gave the horses and mules a day's rest. By evening they returned without having found the camp. The next morning the three men were on their way again and this time they let me come along. Once more Sydney told them where to look for the place. We had one horse and the dogs with us. We hiked for miles over mountains, swamps, tundra and crossed small streams, looking for trees with notches cut in them that marked his trail. Finally we found them and kept them in sight as we moved right along.

"I hope we did not pass the camp," said Jeff, the packer, "It must be around here some place. All of you wait here and I will ride the horse as I can see better over all of this wilderness. I would be a bad packer if I could not find an old camp." He then mounted the horse and rode away. Before long we heard him shout, "I think I have found it as I can see the top of an easel sticking out of the bushes. Yes, it is the right place; there are boxes here with Sydney's name on them." We stayed just long enough to have lunch and then we returned to Poor Man's Creek to tell Sweety the good news.

The next day Jeff, Dick and Arthur loaded the horses and mules and went on their way, leaving Sydney and me behind. After they reached the place they busied themselves by putting up the tents under a few pine trees which were growing at the edge of the timberline. After the work was done Jeff asked Arthur to stay there overnight and keep one of the dogs for company. When we arrived next day Arthur was very glad to see us. He said he was never so scared in his whole life as he was being alone in that great wilderness. "I will never spend another night by myself like this one again."

There were four tents put up. One was ten feet by fourteen feet for living quarters, two tents eight feet by ten feet for sleeping rooms and one six feet by eight feet for storage. Sweety and Arthur cut off small pine twigs and scattered them around the floor of the tents and covered them with tarpaulins and set up the cots on which we placed the sleeping bags.

In the big tent they put a small Yukon stove on which I did all of the cooking and baking. The rest of our furniture consisted of a card table and folding chairs. We were well set up and very comfy. Between sketching, cooking and baking French bread, I was kept very busy and the summer went only too, too fast.

Right behind the camp there was a beautiful stream with swiftly running cold water. The small tent was put up near the creek under the shade of the pines. This was where we kept our supplies and we were well provided.

Sunday dinner was always a chicken dinner with mushrooms, coming out of a can naturally. I made a nice fricassee sauce and home made noodles. As a vegetable, I often picked the tops of fern which was similar to spinach; it was very tasty. Otherwise we had canned vegetables.

About the third week that we were there it began raining and it lasted almost three days. Looking out of the tent I saw a large puddle of water and in the center a little old mouse struggling to get out. Quickly I ran to the rescue, took the poor little mouse in and dried it off, rubbed it with Baume Bengue, laid it in a small box of cotton and set it behind the stove to keep warm. Another mouse came to see her, and in their language, she must have asked the rescued one how she was and the answer must have been, "I am well taken care of." The next day I had her in my lap giving her a massage which she seemed to enjoy immensely. More and more mice arrived, like visitors, looked in the box and chatted with her. Finally they all stayed and made themselves at home. My family of mice increased to forty eight. They ran all over the place. I cooked oatmeal, farina, rice and gave them cheese and leftovers. When time came to leave I asked Sweety what I should do with the mice. He told me just to leave them there and when they got hungry they would find food for themselves and would not starve.

We had quite a few bears around the camp and one of them became quite friendly. Often at night he would come and scratch on the tent and I would scratch back and talk with him. Sweety said, "Kid, don't start feeding him or we will not have food for long." I promised not to. Sydney and Arthur made up their minds to shoot him the first time he came and I was not around. One day he came walking between the tents. Both grabbed their guns and shot him right between the eyes. Both shots were well aimed and hit him only one inch apart. They said they just could not have him hanging around the camp.

Arthur said he would like to have his pelt. "May I skin him?" I asked Sweety. He got a kick out of that and laughingly said, "Sure Kid, go to it." He wondered what I would do or how I could handle it. He was very surprised when he saw me starting right on the inner side of the legs. After watching me for awhile he wanted to know how I learned to skin a wild animal. I said, "In France, my father and uncles often went hunting and came home with a deer or wild boar." I had watched my uncle skinning them and one day asked if he would let me do it. He said I could and after watching me for awhile my uncle said, "You are doing a fair job. I think from now on I will let you do it." After that when they came home with wild game it was my job to dress it out.

We did not have the proper salt with us for curing the hide so Arthur stretched it between two pine trees. He made a comb and combed the fur every day but when the rains started it rotted the pelt so it could not be used.

Every afternoon Sydney and Arthur took a little nap. Often I would go for a hike up the hill. One day when they awoke and did not find me around they were worried that I was lost. Both started calling my name. I was quite a distance up on the mountain which was covered with a thick growth of Alder bushes. I had to part them so I could yell, "Here I am. I'm coming down." Reaching them I got a good scolding. Sweety never wanted me to take a walk by myself as there were too many wild animals around as bears, wolves, foxes and many others. I was never afraid. Sweety worried more about me bringing one of these wild creatures into camp and taming it for a pet than he did about me getting lost.

When I returned to camp after being in the tangle of bushes, Arthur, looked at me and said, "Sit down here on this stump." I did and he got the scissors and chopped my hair off and I do mean 'chopped' it off. He cut it every which way. "I was tired of seeing your hair hanging in the bushes." After the cutting was done he looked at me and laughed, saying to Sydney, "What a perfect beauty we brought along and what a hell of a mess we have made out of her." Sweety laughed and said, "You really did!" As soon as we got back to Anchorage I went to a barber for a haircut. He looked at me and asked, "Whom did you let get at your hair?" "Our camp man did this job," I replied.

With September here it was time to break up camp. We had to wait for the packer. Every day Sydney and Arthur would take the binoculars and look at a far mountain to see if they could spot Jeff coming. "What are you boys doing? Trying to look a hole in the mountain?" They said, "We are looking for the packer to come. It is already the middle of September and the snow is not far off. You don't know, Kid, but if we get snowed in we would never get out of here before the middle of winter and we do not have enough food left to keep us alive that long.

One morning, looking in the same direction on the mountain that they had always looked, I saw Jeff with a horse and the mules. "Hey Sweety," I cried, "here comes Jeff." "Where?" he asked. "Over the mountain where you always look." "That is not possible; you cannot see that far." "Yes, I can. He has a horse and the mules."

Sweety took the binoculars and looked and said, "Art, she is right. There he comes. What an eyesight my Kid has!" It is true that I have excellent eyesight, seeing distant objects very clearly as well as those that are close. I have never worn glasses except for very tedious work.

Nearly everything was packed and the tents were down when Jeff arrived about two hours later. He was surprised to find everything ready. "I did not think you would be set to leave and I brought only one horse. I just came to find out when you wanted to get away from here." We told him that we wanted to leave immediately as we felt it might snow any time and we did not want to be caught in it.

"Sweety, you had better ride the horse and I will walk as it hurts me more to ride than walk." The mules were loaded and ready to go. As Sweety mounted the horse he turned to me and said, "Now Kid, when you see a bear turn around and go the other way."

Arthur and I walked together. We had walked less than four miles when a big Brownie came out of the bushes. "Now what are we going to do?" asked Arthur, "We surely cannot turn back. Where would we go?" "First of all keep your gun on your shoulder. Just stay still and see what the bear will do," I replied. Luckily the bear turned in the same direction as we were walking and we followed very slowly. When he stopped we stopped. Finally he turned and walked toward the river and when we passed him he was slapping fish out of the water. The rest of the day was uneventful just walking up hill and down from one mountain to another.

. . . by *JEANNE LAURENCE*

Toward evening we arrived at Poor Man's Creek where we stayed two days. Jeff had to go back to pick up the rest of our belongings. When he returned from his first trip he said, "You just got out in time. I found two inches of snow." He unloaded and went right back for the rest of our things.

The next morning we started for Dick Francis' cabin where we would wait for Jeff to return with the second load. We found Dick in a bad way. While walking through raspberry bushes one of the twigs hit him in the eye. He rubbed his eyes and the little thorns blinded one eye entirely. he asked if we would take him with us so that he could see a doctor.

The following day we had a forty-two mile trip ahead of us. We started at five o'clock in the morning and walked all day without once stopping to rest or eat. Jeff said to Sydney, "If this woman walks the whole way without complaining I will certainly take my hat off to her." There were no complaints from me.

We had four rivers to cross. The first three Arthur carried me across as he had high hip boots. The third river we had almost crossed when Arthur yelled, "Quicksand! I'll throw you across so hang on to whatever you can grab." Through the air I flew catching on to a bush with my legs hanging in the water. He lay flat down on the water and so escaped sinking.

For the next river we waited for the horse and let him carry us across. The river was about thirty feet wide and water was quite deep so the horse had to swim.

Hiking along I suddenly heard a bear growl behind us. I turned and saw a big Brownie on his hind legs. Doing things by instinct, I growled back. "You learned that very well, you two," Dick said, thinking that Arthur and I were growling at each other. "No, Dick, you are wrong. He is right behind us and don't you touch that gun." The bear kept on growling and I growled too. Finally he made a soft sound like gr, gr, gr, and got on his feet and walked away.

"See Dick," I said, "just talk their language and you get along swell with them." Now I caught it! "Of all the damn fool women I have ever run across you are the biggest. When a bear growls it is time to shoot." Catching up with Sydney, Dick said, "Did you know what your wife did? She actually stayed there growling at a bear." "That's my Jeanne. Nothing surprises me that she is doing. She seems to have a way with animals and a way to tame them."

We kept pushing along and about four in the afternoon we arrived at mile fifty eight at the Road Commissioner's cabin, where Jeff had left the wagon. Next day after loading and leaving everything behind that was not needed we started on. Now there was room enough for Dick and me to stretch. When we arrived at mile twenty eight we found three prospectors waiting to make the trip to Talkeetna. Among them was our Swiss friend.

Early in the morning we set out for the last twenty four miles. During this part of the journey another incident took place. After we had ridden about sixteen miles, Jeff stopped the horse and gave a loud whistle and started up the hill. "What is going on?" I asked Sweety. "Just watch and see," he replied. Before long I saw a man with a barrel strapped on his back and in each hand he was carrying a five gallon jug. He was followed by a beautiful black Newfoundland dog. Now I got the picture; the man made moonshine up in the mountains. Seemingly a good brand which was aged for a year in the ground. I did not taste it myself but all of the men took a swig. Sweety did not want any but they forced the jug on him and he put it to his lips but did not swallow. By the time we got to camp the men had had quite a few snifters and started to feel pretty good. When I saw this I said to Sweety, "I will sleep in the wagon tonight."

When the fellows heard me say that they asked, "Aren't you afraid of the bears?" "No, not as much as I am of you fellows. I fear you will be quite noisy and I want to sleep."

During the night the Swiss fellow, who was the only one besides Sydney who was sober, got up every so often and lit a match and held it over each man to find out if he was all right. "Go see if the woman in the wagon is all right. We are," they would tell him. Everytime he would wake me. Finally I said, "Please do not come anymore. I would like to sleep."

The last day of our journey we were only two miles from the river where the boat was waiting to row us across. On the way to the river Jeff said, "I think it would be a good idea to hide the barrel and the jugs in the woods until we see if the coast is clear as there are always snoopers hanging around to see if there is any bootleg whiskey smuggled in." Sure enough, when we came to the river we found a government agent. He asked us if we knew of a place up in the mountains where they brewed bootleg whiskey; he also asked us if we had any objections to his checking our belongings. To both questions we answered, "No."

After inspecting everything he wanted to know if there were a place around there where he could spend the night and stay a couple of days. Jeff gave him the location of the camp. We were all glad that he chose not to return on the same boat with us.

Now came the portion of the trip which I did not like and that was to cross the rivers in a small boat. I am afraid of water and I cannot swim. We had three rivers to cross. After crossing the first river, Jeff said, "Jeanne, if you want to walk across this island to the other side we will pick you up." This I chose to do. Arthur and two other men walked with me. Coming around a bend we saw Jeff with one foot in the boat and one on a rock hollering at us to stand where we were and shouting very loudly, "There is quicksand that you have to cross over. Now listen carefully. Come in running as swiftly as your feet can carry you and I will catch you." "Be sure that you do," I yelled back. That was the strangest feeling I ever experienced, not having solid ground under my feet. It felt like walking on air.

We arrived in Talkeetna safe and sound. As there was only one train a week, we had to wait for the train to take us back to Anchorage. By the end of September we started on our way back to Los Angeles, California.

Sydney returned with so many orders that it kept him busy throughout the winter. I went sketching every weekend with a group of artist friends. Sweety came with us only a few times. Altogether he painted eight California scenes. California scenery did not appeal too much to him. Furthermore there were so many artists who were trying to make a living and he had more orders for Alaskan scenery than he could handle. He left the California scenery to the California artists. There were but a few artists found in Alaska during the early years.

In March of 1930 we got ready for a trip back to Alaska. We drove our car from Los Angeles to Seattle and from there we took a boat to Juneau where we spent two months sketching and painting. One day while sitting in a cow pasture sketching, Sydney who had chosen a spot about thirty feet from me saw a cow coming toward me and he thought, "Now here is where I will have some fun with Jeanne." He was very sure I would jump up and upset my easel and paints and run but I fooled him. As the cow neared me I looked up and said, "Hi pet, what do you want? Are you going to help me paint?" By that time the cow started to lick my face. Ouch, what a feeling having that scratchy and slimy tongue going over my face. Sweety just laughed and laughed. Still laughing he walked over to me and said, "I expected everything to fly through the air and you taking it on the run. Instead you calmly sat there and let the cow kiss you." "Yes," I said, "and you should have experienced the feeling it gave me. I had shivers running down my spine to my toes."

During the month of June we left Juneau for Cordova, Valdez, Seward and Anchorage, our last stop, where we spent the rest of the summer and part of the autumn. Autumn is the nicest season of the year with its golden colored leaves and red leaf bushes.

By October we were ready to again leave for Los Angeles, which was a wrong move. There was a depression on in the states and things looked very bad, especially for the artists. Sydney had a large order list and thought that we would get by, never dreaming that everyone would cancel their order. Every letter that came brought a cancellation. He would always ask me to open the letters and let him know what was said. Many would say, "We do not want to cancel our order but please wait until we give you further notice and times get better again."

Like ever so many people we lost everything. Sweety and I were wondering what to do next when a letter came from Adolph Schmidt of Seattle, owner of the Washington Hotel, with an invitation to come to Seattle as his guests until times got better again. He said, "I will have a studio, a gallery and a bedroom ready for you."

Adolph Schmidt was a very close friend of Sydney's and knowing what a hard pull artists had during those trying times he came to our rescue, for which we were so very grateful. We accepted his invitation and packed up our belongings and drove to Seattle.

Sydney and Adolph got acquainted through a yacht race which took place between Seattle and Juneau, Alaska. At the time we were in Juneau where we had a studio. The Simpsons, owners of the Nugget Shop, told Sydney of the coming yacht race and asked him if he would paint a canvas to offer as first prize to the winner of the race. "Sure I will; that is a splendid idea," he replied

Right away Sydney began painting a seascape with Indian boats racing to the "Potlatch." He called the painting "On to the Potlatch." The Potlatch was a yearly event. One tribe of Indians would go to visit another tribe exchanging gifts, having dances, playing games and feasting. These shindigs lasted as long as a week or longer.

Adolph Schmidt's yacht, "Winniepeck," won the race and was presented with the painting. At this time he was introduced to Sydney. The two men were instantly attracted to each other and became fast friends. Thinking of Sydney, during these difficult times and wondering how we were making out, the thought came to him to write and invite us to come to Seattle and stay at the hotel until things got better. He let Sydney have one large sample room with an adjoining bedroom on the fourteenth floor. The gallery was on the mezzanine where we exhibited the paintings and where I was the attendant.

A large Mount McKinley painting, six by twelve feet, graced the center wall of the gallery. All in all there were about twenty two paintings of various sizes representing land and seascapes. Each of them a work of art.

Early one morning about eight o'clock the desk clerk called me to the phone. He asked me to go down to the gallery saying there were about thirty five tourists waiting to talk to me about the paintings. I rushed down and greeted them, introducing myself. There were many questions asked.

One lady approached me and looking at the Mount McKinley painting said, "How beautifully he faked the foreground." Thinking that I had not heard right, I asked her to repeat what she had said; she made the same remark again.

"Lady, that foreground is not faked but is just as nature put it there." She looked me straight in the eye and said, "You are a liar!" I started to laugh and said, "I can see that you were never in Alaska." A gentleman, standing nearby listening to the conversation, said to her, "You had better take back what you just called the lady. What you see in that painting is as true as can be; it could not be presented any better. I should know for I spent four months in Alaska one summer. All of those paintings you see hanging are just as true in color and scenery of Alaska as only a master could portray them." The lady looked at me very sheepishly and said, "And I am a school teacher telling my pupils that Alaska is nothing but ice and snow."

After they had gone I went up to Sweety's studio and told him of the occurrence. "One of the women in the group called me a liar as she did not believe that Alaska had four seasons. She thought there was nothing but ice and snow all the year around." Sweety had a good laugh saying, "That shows you what people know about Alaska."

Suddenly, I had an inspiration. "You know, Sweety, what I am going to do when we go back to Alaska? I am going to make a study of the Alaskan flora and illustrate them for a book as there are not any books on the wild flowers of Alaska." "That is a marvelous idea, Kid, go to it."

In the spring of 1934, after things got better, Sweety and I decided to go back to Alaska. We left Seattle in the month of April making our usual stops. We arrived at Anchorage by the end of May and took over our old studios in the Anchorage Hotel.

Now began the season of the wild flowers. I began by searching for them. They were not hard to find as there were ever so many species throughout all of Alaska. It took me twenty years to assemble and make studies of the wild flowers throughout the country. Every year in the spring I flew to a different part of Alaska from Ketchikan up to the Bering Sea. I gathered all kinds of flowers bringing the amount to three hundred species of Alaskan flora. The studies are all painted on a black background.

With the depression over plenty of tourists came to Anchorage and visited Sydney's studio. Many bought paintings which kept him busy. He had more than he could handle and he was very happy. There followed quite a few wonderful years. The only thing wrong was they passed too quickly.

In the year of 1940 Sweety did not feel too well. He said that old age was creeping up on him. He complained that he felt so tired and pepless. I would say to him, "Please, Sweety, lay your paint and brushes aside and rest for awhile and take it easy. Do not worry about anything." That was easily said. He read a lot and worried about the situation our country was in. With the war going on in Europe he was sure that we would be forced into it and he felt we were not prepared.

He would often say, "Why doesn't our President wake up to the facts and get ready. We are going to be jabbed in the back and it won't be by the Russians but will be by the Japanese." His predictions were only too true.

"I am not young enough," said Sweety, "to participate in the war theater and be a war correspondent as I've been before. That is the trouble with getting old; one is no good for anything any more."

The hardest and saddest day of my entire life was September eighth of the same year. Sydney got up as he did every morning at seven o'clock, took his bath, dressed and had breakfast. After breakfast was over he said to me, "Kid, I am going to the barber to have a shave and hair trim."

Arriving at the barber shop he said to the barber, "Give the old boy a good shave and haircut; it will be the last one." "What are you saying there, Sydney?" "Exactly what I meant," was his answer. "Oh, go on. I'll bet I will give you many more after this one." After the barber had finished. Sydney looked in the mirror, saluted and made a funny face at himself saying, "Goodbye, old boy, that is your last shave and haircut."

Leaving the barber shop, Sydney went to the drugstore looking for Esther Able whose husband was the owner of the drugstore. She had purchased a painting of the "Northern Lights" for a Christmas gift for her husband. She had asked Sydney to keep it for her until that time, which he had promised to do. Finding her he said, "Esther, do you want to buy the painting from me?" "Certainly I want to buy it from you. Don't you sell it again like you've done twice before. You know it is to be Bill's Christmas gift." "Then you had better come today as this is my last day on earth," said Sydney. "What are you talking about, Sydney? Are you getting childish? I'll bet you will outlive us. I'll get the painting on Christmas and from you."

Twice he had had a painting of the "Northern Lights" put aside for Esther when tourists, visiting his studio, saw them and insisted on buying them. No other painting would do as that was just what they wanted. Sydney would think, "All right, I will let them have it and I will paint another one for Mrs. Able." That was what Esther had in mind when she said to Sweety, "Don't you sell it again to someone else."

Before going back to his studio Sweety came to see me. Staying behind me and pulling my hair through his fingers he said, "Kid, I am mighty proud of you. You have worked hard going slowly up the ladder step by step; now you are over the last rung and you will always make it. Now I can close my eyes in peace. This is my last day on earth."

"Oh, no! You must not talk like that. I want you to stay with me for many, many years and see the completion of the wildflower book. I think you are just tired and do not feel too well today."

"You bet I am tired. I have no pain but I feel life slowly oozing out of my body." With those words he left me and went to his studio.

Now Sweety had me more and more worried. I could not paint. I said to our little dog, Cossette, "Let's go and see daddy and find out what he is doing." He was not in his studio but we found him in the lobby talking with our friend Flavilla Reckard who was a nurse. When little Cossette spied Sydney she jumped in his lap and kissed him like she had never done before. "See! Your dog knows better what is going to happen than all of you want to believe."

After I went back to my studio, he asked Flavilla if she would stand by in his last hours. "Sure I will. The only thing you need is a rest and you will be all right."

He asked if one could have a private room with bath in the hospital. She told him one could have a private room with all the conveniences one desired. "That is what I am going to do," he replied.

He returned to my studio and asked me to call the hospital and have a room reserved for him, saying, "The hotel doesn't like stiffs hanging around."

I went to the phone and called the hospital. I talked with a Sister and made arrangements for a room. That done I called the doctor and told him how Sydney felt and that he wanted to go to the hospital. "Good! Let me know when he is settled and I will see him right away."

By four o'clock he was comfortably settled in a nice room at the hospital. As I was leaving to go home, he took me in his arms, kissed me and said, "Goodbye, Kid, this is the last time I will see you." "No, I'll be back right after dinner and stay with you during visiting hours."

That night I could not sleep. I got up real early, took a bath and got ready to go to the hospital to find out how he rested. It was six thirty when the phone rang and they told me to come quickly to the hospital as Sydney was not as good as he should be. I called a taxi and went to the hospital. I found him in a coma. Flavilla and a Sister were there attending him. He did not recognize me when I spoke to him. I looked in desperation at Flavilla; she said, "Sweety is slowly slipping away." Ten minutes later he was gone to the great beyond.

Later on Flavilla said that she had never seen anyone leave this earth with such grace and dignity. Like he lived so he died.

And so ended the life of a great man.

Story of a Harem

While in Paris studying at the Beaux Arts, Sydney often went sketching with his friend, Ernest Shaw, who was also a student at the same school.

"What are we going to do during the Easter vacation?" asked Ernest.

"Let's go to Algiers, Africa and make a few studies," which they did.

Walking around the narrow streets of Algiers, Sydney said, "I wish they would leave one of those big doors open so we could sneak in and make a sketch of the beautiful harem ladies."

It was no sooner said than Sydney spied one door slightly ajar. "There is one; let's go in and try our luck." Inside there was a big pool with harem ladies in small gondolas floating around and others just sitting around relaxing. Sydney's and Ernest's eyes nearly popped when they saw all of this beauty.

As Sydney recounted it afterward: "We set up our paintbox and were ready to sketch when suddenly two hands grabbed us by the collar and the seat of our pants and threw us into the middle of the street, paintbox, paints and brushes flying after us. I looked up and saw an eight feet tall eunuch standing over me, saying in perfect English, 'Don't you ever try that again.' Very sheepishly I looked up at him and said, 'Indeed we won't.'"

And so ended their dream to paint the beautiful ladies of the harem.

Story of Father Hubert, The Flying Priest

Father Hubert owned his own plane and had a great love for flying. From time to time he came to visit with Sydney at his studio. One day he walked into the studio and said, "Sydney, get ready and I will take you up in my plane and fly you over Mount Katmai. You can look down in the crater and see what a hole it blew out at the time you were not too far away and lost everything but your skin."

Sydney looked at him and said, "Father, did you ever see a tomato roll off the table?"

"Yes, I have."

"What did it do to it?"

"It smashed it to bits."

"Well then, I will stay right here on mother earth and keep solid ground under my feet. I don't want to come down like a smashed tomato."

And that was that. Sydney just would not be convinced of a safe return.

Story of a Poet

One day a lady tourist came to visit Sydney's studio. Looking around at all of the beautiful paintings on the wall she said, "What a wonderful gift God gave you, to go into this beautiful setting of nature and represent it in its true color. It could not be reproduced more perfectly. You must be very proud."

Sydney looked at her and said, "All artists are a little nutty but the one who is nuttier than an artist is a poet."

Astonished at the remark she said, "Thanks very much, I have just published my first book of poetry."

With a twinkle in his eye, Sydney looked at her and said, "What I just said still goes."

She laughed and said, "I accept it. Please promise me that when you and your wife come to Seattle that you will telephone and come and have dinner with me."

We did give her a ring on the phone, and had a nice dinner and spent a pleasant evening visiting with her.

Meeting the Train

In the early days of Alaska there was but one train a week. Many people went to see the train come in, Sydney and Rusty Heurlin among them. Rusty was a very close friend of Sydney and also an excellent artist. He painted the life of the Eskimos, showing many scenes of Point Barrow and surroundings which were a very good portrayal of the early history of Alaska.

Both were standing by the train when a Colonel Emery got off. As he descended he noticed Sydney standing there and he said to him, "A lovely country you've got here."

Sydney's reply was, "It is a hell of a country. In the summer it is light twenty four hours a day and in the winter they can track you."

Turning to Rusty the Colonel asked, "Who is that fellow over there? He has a great sense of humor."

"That is Sydney Laurence, the famous painter," he replied.

Personalities

Quite a few persons of note visited Sydney's studio. One of them was President Herbert Hoover, who spent an hour chatting with him and at the same time bought five of his paintings.

When Will Rogers flew Wiley Post to Alaska they made a stop at Anchorage. Both came to Sydney's studio to visit. Will Rogers took a great liking to him and for four hours they were pitting their wits against each other.

Sydney kidded Rogers for taking a chance by flying with Wiley Post in such a small plane, over such rough terrain and under such unpredictable weather conditions.

When they parted, Will Rogers said, "On our way back we will stop over again. We will see you and pick up some paintings."

The next day they flew to Fairbanks and stayed over night. On the morning of August fifteenth, 1935, they took off for Point Barrow. About fourteen miles south of Point Barrow they crashed and lost their lives.

Rear Admiral Kuntz had twelve Senators and the Secretary of the Interior, Tom Sayer (who was a close friend of ours) on his ship. They left the boat at Seward and took the train to Anchorage.

The first thing Tom Sayer did was call on us. He said to me, "Jeanne, get ready and prepare a dinner for fourteen people. I've invited all the Senators and Rear Admiral Kuntz to dinner, telling them they should look forward to an excellent meal."

I got busy right away and by six thirty I had dinner ready. Everyone seemed to enjoy his dinner very much and I was complimented on my excellent cooking.

After dinner the Admiral asked me, "When do you have breakfast?" I replied, "About eight o'clock." "And what time is lunch and dinner?" he asked. I told him lunch was at noon and dinner about six thirty. "Good, that will suit me," he replied.

I thought that he was kidding. The next morning at eight o'clock there came a knock at the door. We were just ready to sit down to breakfast. Quickly Sweety got another setting on the table. Slowly I went to the door and opened it.

"Ah, good morning. You are just in time for breakfast," I greeted him.

After we were through eating he said, "I will be here for lunch."

He had breakfast, lunch and dinner with us during the entire time the senators were in Alaska, which was six days. He said, "Where ever I can find a good home-cooked meal that is where I can be found."

Tom Sayer always had dinner with us when he was in town.

There was but one restaurant in town. Although Anchorage was the largest town in Alaska at that time it had a population of only 4800 people.

Publisher's Note

We proudly present reproductions of many Sydney Laurence paintings, which tell so much about the interests and character of the "Great Man."

Gathering and collecting the transparencies from which these reproductions were made was a big chore, but Jeanne Laurence approached it with her usual dauntless courage and energy. The paintings shown are from private and museum collections all over the West.

In some cases Jeanne took a photographer right into the homes of the owners of the paintings, to get transparencies for this book. Conditions were not always completely favorable for picture taking, and some had to be discarded, so that only pictures worthy of the original paintings would be shown. Some transparencies were too small (only 35mm) to enlarge to page size and still do justice to the painting. Because of our desire to show as much of Laurence's work as possible, these pictures are grouped in almost catalogue fashion at the end of the collection.

We felt that no comment on our part was necessary or appropriate, as each picture carries it own message to the individual viewer. In brief, they speak for themselves.

The paintings Laurence did in England and Venice are in the front of the section. Generally, the rest of the paintings are grouped according to subject, as there was no way to be absolutely sure of their chronology.

Much credit should be given Jeanne's friend Herbert S. Green, who assisted her in collecting the transparencies, and who, according to his own statement, is a nut on Sydney Laurence.

Laurence painted the crucifixion, the first painting in the section, on learning of the death of his son in World War I. Mr. Green's sensitive comment about his feeling on viewing it shows an understanding of Laurence and his paintings.

Albert P. Salisbury

106 SELECTED PAINTINGS FROM THE BRUSH OF SYDNEY LAURENCE

"I have been thinking for some good while just how to express my feelings in connection with this picture and really how deep can a person go only to say, this is how a really artistic soul of a man has expressed the deep sorrow over the loss of his son. As the truth goes Sydney Laurence endured much tragedy and misfortune in his life time, but as a person who kept so much inside of himself, it is a miracle beyond words, how he expressed himself so beautifully on canvas. This picture gives the viewer a feeling for the strong religious side of him."

Herbert S. Green, Jr.

THE CRUCIFIXION, Courtesy of The Hamilton Aaris Collection.

MOUNT McKINLEY, Courtesy the Whitney Gallery of Western Art.

SELF PORTRAIT, Courtesy The Frye Art Museum.

AN OLD ENGLISH LANDSCAPE, Courtesy The Frye Art Museum.

PASTORAL LAND SCAPE, Courtesy The Charles Soderstrom Collection.

70

LIGHTHOUSE, Courtesy The Charles Soderstrom collection.

VENETIAN
FISHING BOATS,
Courtesy Anonymous.

72

VENETIAN FISHING BOATS, Courtesy the Schmidt Family.

OUTWARD BOUND FROM VENICE, Courtesy The Charles Soderstrom Collection.

CLIPPER BARKENTINE, Courtesy Temple Smith. (*Reproduced from a print by Herbert S. Green.*)

THE BARKENTINE, Courtesy the Schmidt Family.

COBWEBS,
Courtesy
Mrs. T. M. Anderson

THE CAVE WOMAN, Courtesy the National Bank of Alaska.

MOUNT McKINLEY, Courtesy Mrs. Mary Brown.

MOUNT McKINLEY, Courtesy The Charles Soderstrom Collection.

80

MT. McKINLEY WATER COLOR, Courtesy Anonymous.

MT. McKINLEY, Courtesy the Schmidt Family.

ALASKA THE BEAUTIFUL, Courtesy the Goldberg Collection.
(Reproduced from a print by Herbert S. Green.)

SUMMER AT MOUNT McKINLEY, Courtesy Ruth Barrack.

MOUNT McKINLEY, Courtesy National Bank of Alaska.

ALASKA'S MOUNT McKINLEY, Courtesy Mr. and Mrs. John Dolginer.

BURNING OFF, Courtesy of Mr. and Mrs. Ted Halton. (*Reproduced from a print by Herbert S. Green.*)

EARLY EVENING GLOW ON MOUNT McKINLEY,
Courtesy Dr. and Mrs. John Weston.

MOUNT McKINLEY, Courtesy Anonymous.

SOME OLD PROSPECTORS HOME, Courtesy The Hamilton Aaris
Collection. *(Reproduced from a Print by Herbert S. Green.)*

ALASKA STEAMSHIP IN SEATTLE HARBOR, Courtesy the Schmidt
Family.

LOADING SALMON, EARLY MORNING, Courtesy Mr. and Mrs. H. W. McCurdy.

92

CLAWING OFF THE LEE SHORE, Courtesy Mr. and Mrs. Jerry Church.

93

CLAWING OFF THE LEE SHORE, Courtesy The National Bank of Alaska.

STEAMER AT CANNERY, Courtesy The Charles Soderstrom Collection.

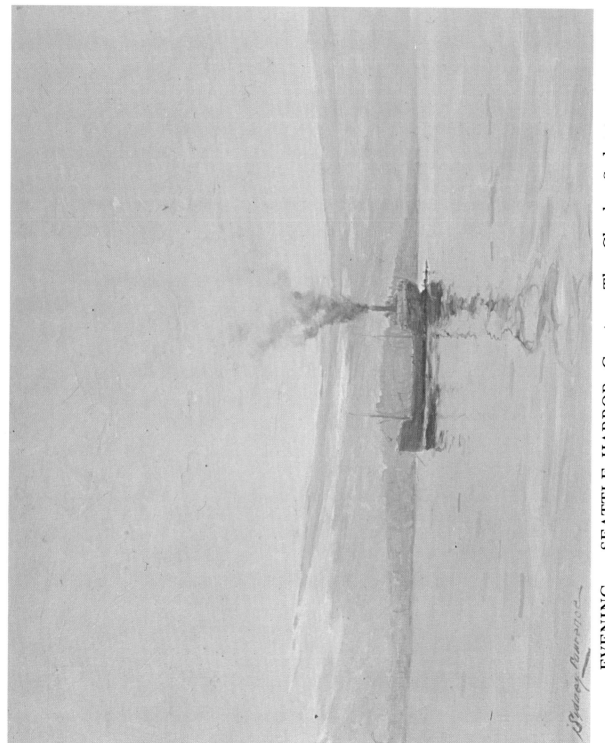

EVENING — SEATTLE HARBOR, Courtesy The Charles Soderstrom Collection.

96

HALIBUT FISHER, Courtesy Senator and Mrs. John Butrovich.

LIFE ON THE YUKON, Courtesy The Charles Soderstrom Collection.

THE WINNIFRED — *The Yacht that won the boat race from Seattle to Juneau, owner Adolph Schmidt, Courtesy the Schmidt Family.*

ALASKA SUNSET, Courtesy The Charles Soderstrom Collection.

BELUGA RIVER CACHE, Courtesy Senator and Mrs. John Butrovich.

101

CACHE BY THE RIVER, Courtesy Harry and Wandine DeVane.

102

INDIAN FISH CACHE, Courtesy Senator and Mrs. John Butrovich.

LUPINE ON THE RICHARDSON HIGHWAY, Courtesy Senator and Mrs. John Butrovich.

CACHE IN THE MOONLIGHT, Courtesy the Schmidt Family.

CACHE ON POORMANS CREEK, Courtesy Mr. and Mrs. Jerry Church.

ALASKAN INDIAN CACHE, Courtesy Mr. and Mrs. Arthur Pedersen. *(Reproduced from a print by Herbert S. Green.)*

INDIAN WOMAN AND FISH CACHE, Courtesy Senator and Mrs. John
Butrovich.

ALASKA AUTUMN AND CACHE, Courtesy Mrs. Mary Brown.

POTLATCH BOUND, Courtesy Mr. and Mrs. John Dolginer.

110

GOING TO THE POTLATCH, Courtesy the Schmidt Family.

ON TO THE POTLATCH, Courtesy Mr. and Mrs. Larry Meath.

THE CASTAWAY, Courtesy the Schmidt Family.

THE NORTHERN LIGHTS, Courtesy the National Bank of Alaska.

THE NORTHERN LIGHTS, Courtesy Harry and Wandine DeVane.

CAPE ST. ELIAS, Courtesy the Schmidt Family.

CAPE ST. ELIAS, Courtesy the National Bank of Alaska.

117

STORM CLOUDS OVER LAKE OTTER, ALASKA, Courtesy
University of Alaska Museum.

RUGGED COAST OF ALASKA, Courtesy National Bank of Alaska.

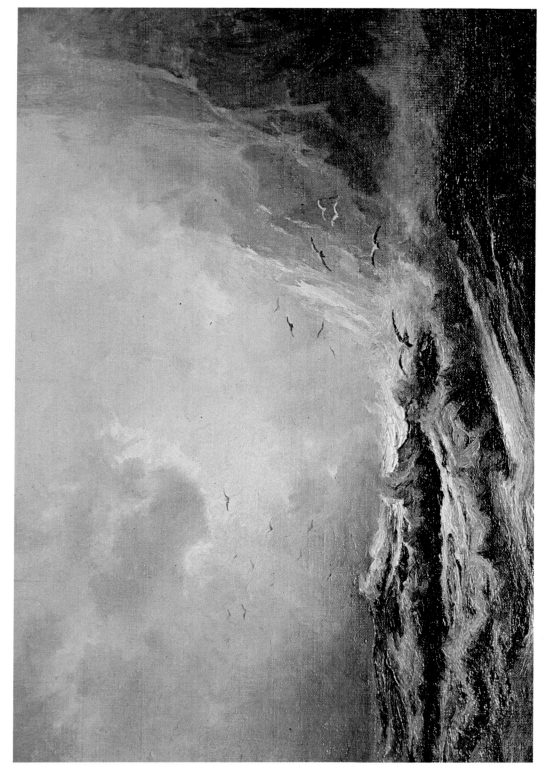

GULLS ALONG THE STORM CLIFFS, Courtesy University of Alaska
Museum.

STORMY SEA COAST, Courtesy Dr. and Mrs. Curtis Johnson.

CASTLE CAPE, Courtesy John Meggitt.

122

CASTLE CAPE, Courtesy National Bank of Alaska.

TRADING POST ON WHISKEY CREEK, Courtesy University of Alaska Museum.

ROAD HOUSE ON THE SUSITNA, Courtesy the Schmidt Family.

OLD SOURDOUGHS HOUSE NEAR SLEEPING INDIAN MOUNTAIN,
Courtesy University of Alaska Museum.

ROAD HOUSE ON THE SUSITNA, Courtesy the Schmidt Family.

OLD SOURDOUGHS HOUSE NEAR SLEEPING INDIAN MOUNTAIN,
Courtesy University of Alaska Museum.

THE TRAPPER, Watercolor, Courtesy of Senator and Mrs. John Butrovich.

127

RELIC OF THE FORGOTTEN PAST, Courtesy Senator and Mrs. John Butrovich.

CABIN IN THE SNOW, Courtesy Ruth Barrack.

CABIN IN THE WILDERNESS, Courtesy The Charles Soderstrom Collection.

CABIN IN THE TREES, Courtesy The Charles Soderstrom Collection.

MOUNT SHUKSAN NEAR MOUNT BAKER NATIONAL PARK, Courtesy
Mr. and Mrs. Jerry Church.

TWILIGHT ON THE SUSITNA RIVER, Courtesy Dr. and Mrs. Haggard.

AUTUMN ON THE RIVER, Courtesy Mrs. Mary Brown.

EVENING GLOW, Courtesy The Charles Soderstrom Collection.

LOW WATER NEAR JUNEAU, ALASKA, Courtesy Mrs. Mary Brown.

DERELICT ROW BOAT ON BEACH WITH MOON OVER ALASKA
WATER, Courtesy University of Alaska Museum.

137

EVENING GLOW, Courtesy Ed Goldfield

138

MENDENHALL GLACIER, Courtesy Mr. and Mrs. Herbert S. Green.

PEARLY DAWN, Courtesy The Charles Soderstrom Collection.

140

TRANQUILITY, Courtesy Dr. and Mrs. John Weston.

141

THE GOLDEN NORTH, Courtesy Harry and Wandine DeVane.

JUNEAU, ALASKA, Courtesy Anonymous.

GASTINEAU CHANNEL, Courtesy Mrs. Mary Brown.

PROSPECTOR'S BOAT, STOPPING FOR LUNCH IN ALASKA, Courtesy
University of Alaska Museum.

ROUGH SEA, Courtesy Anonymous.

ALASKA HUSKY NEAR TENT, Courtesy Charles Soderstrom Collection.

147

WINTER SCENE WITH CABIN, Courtesy Senator and Mrs. John Butrovich.

SNOW SCENE NEAR ANCHORAGE, Courtesy Anonymous.

ON THE TRAIL, ALASKA WINTER, Courtesy Dr. and Mrs. John Weston.

WINTER SCENE, Courtesy National Bank of Alaska.

PTARMIGAN IN WINTER, Courtesy Ray and Tonie Petersen.

152

ALASKA TRAIL, Courtesy Mr. and Mrs. Herbert S. Green.

DUCK HUNTER, Courtesy Senator and Mrs. John Butrovich.

THE DUCK HUNTER, Courtesy The Charles Soderstrom Collection.

THE TRAPPER, Courtesy Ed Olson

156

MOUNT McKINLEY, Courtesy Mr. and Mrs. Robert Atwood.

ICE BOUND, Courtesy Clifford Dolph — the Maryhill Museum.

FOOD CACHE, Courtesy Mr. and Mrs. Robert Atwood.

AUTUMN ON AUKE LAKE, Courtesy Marie Schodde.

FIELD OF IRIS NEAR JUNEAU, Courtesy Dr. and Mrs. Lloyd Hines.

WINTER SUNSET IN ALASKA, Courtesy Dr. and Mrs. Asa Martin.

NORTHERN LIGHTS, Courtesy Marie Schodde.

CAPE ST. ELIAS, Courtesy Mr. and Mrs. Earl Tuter.

PRINCE GEORGE WAR BOAT, Courtesy Jeanne Laurence (the only one of Sydney's paintings Jeanne still owns).

INDIAN HOME WITH TOTEM, Courtesy Dr. and Mrs. Lloyd Hines.

THE TRAPPER, Courtesy, Clifford Dolph —
the Maryhill Museum.

SAILING SHIP ON THE HIGH SEAS OF
ALASKA, Courtesy Dr. and Mrs. Lloyd Hines.

SLOUGH NEAR COOK INLET, Courtesy
Ray and Tonie Petersen.

SQUAW MAN, Courtesy Clifford Dolph —
the Maryhill Museum.

Often Sydney made a small pencil sketch preliminary to making the final painting. As shown this was originally titled "Old Cabin in the Hills," it was shown in the last major Laurence exhibit at the Frye Art Museum in Seattle, a reproduction of the final painting appears on page 60.